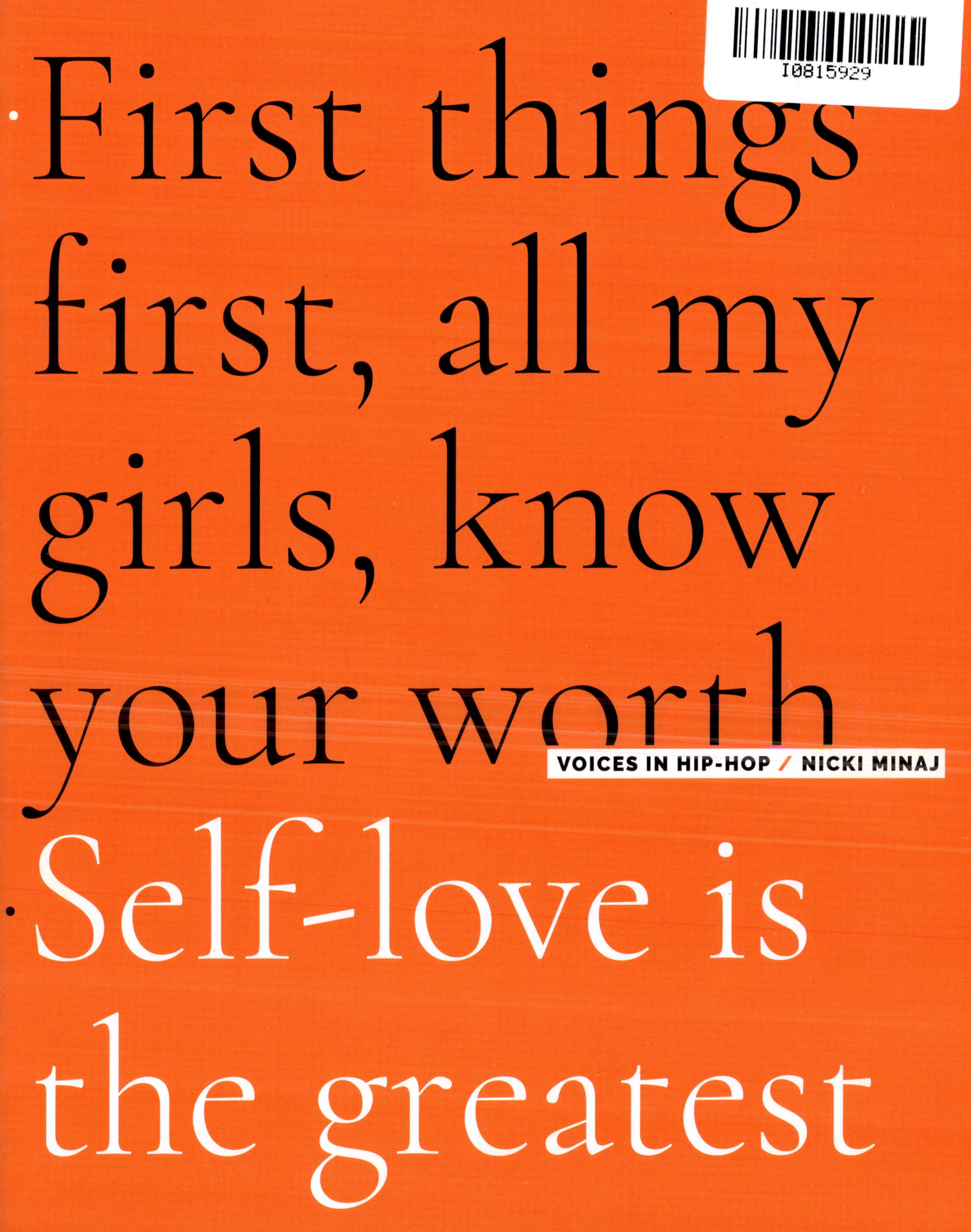
First things first, all my girls, know your worth
VOICES IN HIP-HOP / NICKI MINAJ
Self-love is the greatest

Barbie

VOICES IN HIP-HOP

NICKI MINAJ

MICHAEL JUDSON BERRY

CREATIVE EDUCATION / CREATIVE PAPERBACKS

Let me tell y

I am, I am co

blister

'Cause

and I'r

And th

Published by Creative Education and Creative Paperbacks
P.O. Box 227, Mankato, Minnesota 56002
Creative Education and Creative Paperbacks are imprints of The Creative Company
www.thecreativecompany.us

Design by Graham Morgan
Art direction by Blue Design (www.bluedes.com)

Images by Dreamstime/Fabio Diena, cover, 3, 22; Getty Images/Brian Rasic, 9, by Marc Guitard, 13, Dimitrios Kambouris, 38, Gregg DeGuire, 46, Jamie McCarthy, 37, 45, Jason LaVeris, 15, Johnny Nunez, 19, Jon Kopaloff, 31, Julia Beverly, 23, Kevin Mazur, 10, 40, 43, Michael Stewart, 27, Michael Tran, 28, Paras Griffin, 16, Prince Williams, 2; Pexels/Roberto Nickson, 32; Wikimedia Commons/Dyllan, 39, Eva Rinaldi, 33, Jen, 4, Zebukan, 29
Every effort has been made to contact copyright holders for material reproduced in this book. Any omissions will be rectified in subsequent printings if notice is given to the publisher.

Library of Congress Cataloging-in-Publication Data
Names: Berry, Michael Judson, author.
Title: Nicki Minaj / by Michael Judson Berry.
Description: Mankato, Minnesota : Creative Education and Creative Paperbacks, 2026. | Series: Voices in hip-hop | Includes index. | Audience: Ages 12–15 | Audience: Grades 7–9 | Summary: "Listen up! It's Nicki Minaj, the outspoken and empowering hip-hop artist. Part biography, part song lyric collection, this music-fueled title for high school readers celebrates the rapper's journey and voice. Includes a selected discography and index"– Provided by publisher.
Identifiers: LCCN 2024050284 (print) | LCCN 2024050285 (ebook) | ISBN 9798889892823 (library binding) | ISBN 9781682776483 (paperback) | ISBN 9798889893936 (ebook)
Subjects: LCSH: Minaj, Nicki–Juvenile literature. | Rap musicians–United States–Juvenile literature.
Classification: LCC ML3930.M313 B47 2026 (print) | LCC ML3930.M313 (ebook) | DDC 782.42164092 [B]–dc23/eng/20241023
LC record available at https://lccn.loc.gov/2024050284
LC ebook record available at https://lccn.loc.gov/202

Printed in India

ou this, sister
der than a

w's so sick,
atic
t be cured

contents

• • •

Foreword 8
Introduction 11
Island Childhood 12
School Days 17
Working It 21
Time to Shine 24
Bling, Bling, Bling 26
Big Screen 30
No Stopping 34
Stuff of Dreams 36
Queen of Hip-Hop 41
Never Stop Learning 44
Selected Works by Nicki Minaj 47
Index 48

VOICES IN
HIP-HOP

Foreword

• • •

"Before the arrival of Nicki Minaj in the late 2000s, only a handful of female rappers had ever released platinum solo albums: Lauryn Hill, Missy Elliott, Lil' Kim, Foxy Brown, Da Brat, Eve. Despite their innovations and artistry—or maybe because of them—the genre had narrow expectations and accommodations for the expression of women, and often pitted them against each other, as if the space for anyone but men was zero-sum.

"If hip-hop wouldn't make room, Minaj would, though. Minaj—a theater kid with a vicious tongue, a fierce freestyler, a polyvalent character actor—definitively broke that stalemate, becoming a pop superstar without having to strictly follow in the footsteps of any of those women."

—JON CARAMANICA, POP MUSIC CRITIC, *THE NEW YORK TIMES*, DECEMBER 13, 2023

Introduction

icki Minaj is one of the greatest musical artists of her generation. She defied the odds from the start, beginning her life on the Caribbean island of Trinidad before immigrating to the United States with her family as a child. Like most kids, Minaj dreamed of a larger, grander life. She sat in her room, inventing new names and personas for herself, writing songs, and imagining what her life could be like if she only had the confidence to go out and demand it. Many people daydream of fame and fortune, but few achieve it. Minaj not only found success in music but also helped redefine the hip-hop genre and paved the way for aspiring future artists.

Minaj is unapologetically bold. Her willingness to take chances and experiment with her appearance and her sound has helped keep her on top with fans and critics alike. It's been 14 years since the self-named "Barbie" debuted her first album, and she shows no signs of slowing anytime soon. In late 2024, Minaj's *Pink Friday 2* took home Hip Hop Album of the Year at the BET Hip Hop Awards, further solidifying this phenomenal woman's right to wear to the crown.

VOICES IN
HIP-HOP

Island Childhood

• • •

"You figure out the value of money when you come from a different country, and then you don't have what the other kids have."

—NICKI MINAJ, *VOGUE*, 2023

Nicki Minaj was born Onika Tanya Maraj on December 8, 1982, in the Republic of Trinidad and Tobago. Her father, Robert, worked as an executive, and her mother, Carol, worked in payroll and accounting. Nicki was the second-oldest of four children, with an older brother and a younger brother and sister. One thing that Nicki's

Trinidad and Tobago

parents had in common was music. They were both gospel singers who instilled a love of music in their children from an early age.

THE COLOR PINK

One color has become so synonymous with Nicki Minaj that some people have jokingly said she invented it: pink. From her clothes, hair, and makeup to her cars, branded shoes, and names of her albums, pink is everywhere. She once told a reporter, "When I was younger, I didn't have much financially, like we couldn't afford a lot of stuff, and I remember seeing little girls' rooms on TV, and they'd all be pink. I didn't have my own room, I shared with my brother, so I would have this daydream and imagine that one day I could have my own room, and it would all be pink, like Cinderella's."

When Nicki was three years old, her parents moved to New York City, hoping to find opportunities to build a different life for the family. Nicki and her siblings were left in Trinidad with their grandmother, along with 11 cousins. In the very full house, Nicki wondered if she would ever see her parents again. In the 2010 *MTV News* documentary *Nicki Minaj: My Time Now*, she said, "A lot of times, when you're from the islands, your parents leave and then send for you because it's easier when they have established themselves, when they have a place to stay, when they have a job . . . I thought it was gonna be for a few days; it turned into two years without my mother."

Finally, when Nicki was five years old, her parents sent for her and her siblings, and the whole family was reunited in South Jamaica, Queens. Nicki expected her new home in the United States to be a castle. It wasn't. But even at a young age, she was ready to work hard and make the most of this new opportunity she was given.

Got a billboard out in Times Square
So when they see me, they say 'Ah, she there!'"

—FROM "POUND THE ALARM," ON THE 2012 ALBUM *PINK FRIDAY: ROMAN RELOADED*

Barbie

School Days

Let me tell you this, sister
I am, I am colder than a blister
'Cause my flow's so sick, and I'm a lunatic
And this can't be cured with no Elixir

—FROM "ROMAN HOLIDAY," ON THE 2012 ALBUM *PINK FRIDAY: ROMAN RELOADED*

Life in the United States wasn't the fairy tale young Nicki had hoped for. The family struggled to make ends meet, and her father faced many personal demons. Opening up about her childhood to *Rolling Stone* in 2010, she revealed, "When I first came to America, I would go in my room and kneel down at the foot of my bed and pray that God would make me rich so that I could take care of my mother."

…You could be the king but watch the queen conqu

…OK first things first

Working It

While at LaGuardia, Minaj immersed herself in all styles of music. She found inspiration from rappers Foxy Brown and Jay-Z. Monica was also one of her greatest influences, along with Beyoncé, Drake, and, most surprisingly, Irish singer Enya. Minaj loved Enya's airiness and whimsy, qualities Minaj used when crafting her own music.

After graduating in 2000, Minaj was ready to pursue her dream of becoming a professional actress. At age 19, she found a bit of success. She booked an off-Broadway production called *In Case You Forget*, a play about teenage graffiti artists.

For the next few years, the aspiring actress worked odd jobs, trying to keep her head above water. Many of them did not end well. Minaj claims she was fired from at least 15 jobs, including Red Lobster, where she was let go for being rude to customers.

The tough, bold, and brash persona that would become a cornerstone of Minaj's future success was already on full display.

The years of working odd jobs only fueled Minaj's desire for fame and fortune. She tirelessly took whatever performing gig she could find, anything to get out in front of an audience. She took backup singing roles for other rappers, while still writing her own songs. She knew the odds were stacked against her. "Female rappers get it the hardest," Minaj said. "You have to be a girl, yet you have to be just as hard as the guys. I think some female rappers get scared out of the business before they can make it." But she also knew if she just kept at it, even when it felt like the whole world was telling her NO, she would make it.

And I will retire with the crown, yes
No, I'm not lucky, I'm blessed, yes
Clap for the heavyweight champ, me
But I couldn't do it all alone, we

—FROM "MOMENT 4 LIFE," ON THE 2010 ALBUM *PINK FRIDAY*

Nicki Minaj and Lil Wayne

Time to Shine

In the early 2000s, Minaj took advantage of the emergence of the Internet as a new way to share music. She began recording her own songs and posting them to her MySpace page. She sent demos to as many people as she could in the music industry. And after a while, all that hard work paid off. She grabbed the attention of Fendi, CEO of the Brooklyn-based music label Dirty Money Entertainment, and in 2007, he signed her.

Over the next two years, Minaj recorded and released three mixtapes: *Playtime Is Over, Sucka Free,* and *Beam Me Up Scotty*. All were well received and even covered on BET and MTV. Her 2009 song "I Get Crazy," featuring fellow rapper Lil Wayne,

hit number 20 on the U.S. Billboard Hot Rap Songs chart and number 37 on the Hot R&B/Hip-Hop Songs chart. Minaj was finally getting the recognition she craved.

Lil Wayne was so impressed with Minaj that he signed her to his music group, Young Money Entertainment, in 2009. Her first solo song, "Your Love," which would later become the lead single for her debut studio album, came in at number 14 on the Billboard charts. It also won her Best Hip Hop Female at the BET Awards. A few months later, on November 19, 2010, Minaj's debut studio album dropped. Called *Pink Friday*, it included duets with some of the biggest names in music, including Drake, Rihanna, Eminem, will.i.am, Kanye West, and Natasha Bedingfield. *Pink Friday* reached number one on Billboard and was the highest-grossing rap album by any female that century. By December, the album had gone platinum, selling more than one million copies.

I fly with the stars, in the skies
I am no longer trying to survive
I believe that life is a prize
But to live, doesn't mean you're alive

—FROM "MOMENT 4 LIFE," ON THE 2010 ALBUM *PINK FRIDAY*

Bling, Bling, Bling

• • •

Minaj had gone from a cramped house in Trinidad to the throne of music royalty. The success of *Pink Friday* not only launched her into hip-hop stardom but also earned her four Grammy nominations, including Best New Artist and Best Rap Album. Minaj was on fire, and she was about to get even hotter.

Pop superstar Madonna, herself a queen of music royalty, was set to perform the Super Bowl XLVI (46) halftime show in February 2012. She had Minaj on her radar and asked the talented up-and-coming artist to perform with her. Minaj, of course, said yes.

She later said that rehearsals had been "the most grueling thing [they had] ever done" but added that the show was an "epic learning experience." By the end of the song "Give Me All Your Luvin,'" alongside Madonna and fellow rapper M.I.A., Minaj had been seen by more than 114 million people around the globe.

Less than a month later, Minaj performed her song "Roman Holiday" at the 2012 Grammy Awards, becoming the first solo female rapper to perform at the ceremony. Then came Minaj's second album, *Pink Friday: Roman Reloaded*. The record debuted at number one on the Billboard 200 in April 2012. It was a massive success, reaching the top of the pop, R&B, and rap charts. Many of its songs became hits, but none was more popular than the dance song "Starships."

Now everybody, let me hear you say ray, ray, ray
Go spend all your money 'cause today payday
And if you're a G, you a G, G, G
My name is Onika, you can call me Nicki (woo)

—FROM "STARSHIPS," ON THE 2012 ALBUM *PINK FRIDAY: ROMAN RELOADED*

Big Screen

As Minaj became more and more successful as a recording artist, she decided to once again pursue acting opportunities. She began with a voice-over role in the 2012 movie *Ice Age: Continental Drift,* the fourth installment of the Ice Age film franchise. Minaj played the role of Steffie, the mammoth. The film was a big hit, becoming the highest grossing animated film of the year.

Minaj's next acting role came in 2014, when she starred opposite Cameron Diaz in the romantic comedy *The Other Woman*. Despite mixed reviews, *The Other Woman* debuted at number one at the box office its opening weekend.

In 2016, Minaj earned a Teen Choice Awards nomination for playing the saucy hair stylist Draya in *Barbershop: The Next Cut*. She found herself in the running alongside top actresses such as Anne Hathaway and fellow LaGuardia alumna Jennifer

HOLLYWOOD
STOP
ONLY

Aniston. The third installment of the hit Barbershop series came in second at the box office its opening weekend and received rave reviews. It currently has a 90 percent approval score on the review website Rotten Tomatoes. The site's critical census says, "Heartfelt, thought-provoking, and above all funny, *Barbershop: The Next Cut* is the rare belated sequel that more than lives up to the standard set by its predecessors."

I'm Meryl Streep to all these b—, they can't do what I do
Sometimes I just look in the mirror and I be like, "Why you?"
Yeah, I know that they mad, but I'm a s— on my critics some more

—FROM "WIN AGAIN," ON THE 2014 ALBUM *THE PINKPRINT*

No Stopping

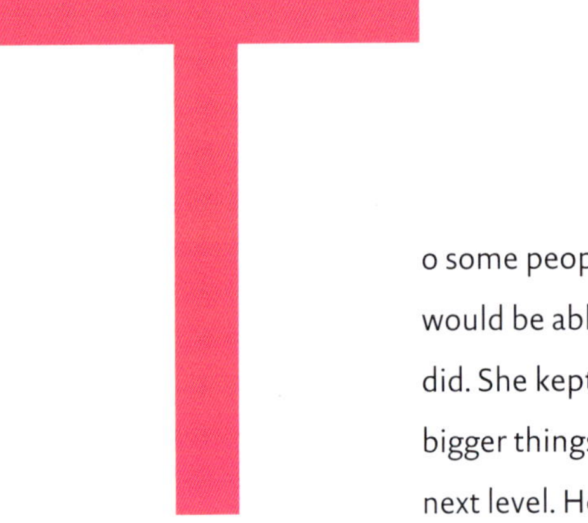

o some people, it seemed impossible that Minaj would be able to top her first two albums. But she did. She kept her eyes forward and kept dreaming of bigger things, pushing to take her music career to the next level. Her third album, *The Pinkprint,* released in 2014. It featured a star-studded list of guest collaborators, including Beyoncé, Chris Brown, Ariana Grande, and Drake. *The Pinkprint* became Minaj's third album in a row to go platinum and won her Best Female Hip Hop Artist at the BET Awards—her fifth consecutive win in that category.

Minaj continued to crank out hit after hit. She was nominated for five more Grammys and broke the record for most entries on the Billboard Hot 100 by a female artist. It was a milestone previously held by the music legend Aretha Franklin.

In 2018, Minaj launched her own radio show called *Queen Radio* for Apple Music Beats 1 station. Just two days later, she released her fourth studio album, *Queen,* which

debuted at number two. Like her previous albums, it went platinum. Minaj kicked off a world tour in early 2019 to promote *Queen*. She dropped many hit singles and collaborated with top recording artists from all around the world. She also lent her voice to the animated film *The Angry Birds Movie 2,* playing a tall, happy bird named Pinky.

Minaj was on top of the world, seeing her music and acting dreams come true. And then she shocked fans with a big announcement. She was taking a break from performing to pursue two new roles: wife and mother.

"S" on my chest 'cause I'm ready to save him
Ready to get buck on anybody that plays him
And I think I love him, I love him just like I raised him
When he call me "mama, lil' mama," I call him "baby"

—FROM "YOUR LOVE," ON THE 2010 ALBUM *PINK FRIDAY*

Stuff of Dreams

In 2019, Minaj married the love of her life, her high school sweetheart, Kenneth Petty. The queen of hip-hop had found her prince. Many celebrities struggle to find people who will love them for who they really are and not because of their fame or wealth. For Minaj, Petty was perfect because he'd grown up with her in the same neighborhood in Queens and still called her by her real name.

The couple welcomed a son, nicknamed "Papa Bear," in 2020. For Minaj, being a mother proved to be equally exciting and nerve-wracking . She found motherhood to be just as scary and fraught with anxiety as any new mother. She later said, "I kind of wish that someone had told me—although I'm sure I wouldn't have been able to understand it—that there's a level of anxiety, and you think it's going to go away,

Nicki Minaj and Kenneth Petty

but in fact, it gets scarier. So often you think: 'I don't know how to do this!'" Despite the fact that many celebrities hire nannies for their children, Minaj refused. "I'm a Trinidadian woman . . . Culturally, we're not really used to nannies and strangers taking care of the babies."

Minaj's own childhood had been marked with struggle, from staying with her grandmother for years before being brought to the United States to growing up in a household full of anger and yelling. Because of those challenging experiences, Minaj wanted to give her child the fairy-tale life she'd dreamed of as a kid. Like with her music, she approached being a parent with passion, determination, and most importantly, love.

See, I need you in my life for me to stay
Know, know, know, know, know, I know you'll stay
No, no, no, no, no, don't go away, hey
Boy, you got my heartbeat runnin' away

—FROM "SUPER BASS," FROM THE 2010 ALBUM *PINK FRIDAY (DELUXE)*

RED RUBY

Queen of Hip-Hop

Starships were meant to fly
Hands up and touch the sky
Can't stop 'cause we're so high
Let's do this one more time, oh

—FROM "STARSHIPS," FROM THE 2012 ALBUM *PINK FRIDAY: ROMAN RELOADED*

hen Minaj chose to put her career on hold and become a mother, she feared she'd never get back on top. She thought motherhood would dim her passion for making

Starships wer

meant to fly

Hands up and

touch the sky

Can't stop

'cause we're so

music. She said there might even have been a part of her that would've been happy to leave music behind. That wasn't the case, though. Songs were in her blood. Minaj needed to work.

As soon as she felt comfortable, Minaj returned to the studio and recorded more hits. Her song "Super Freaky Girl" debuted in 2022 at number one on Billboard 100, her third U.S. number-one hit. The following year, she released her fifth studio album, *Pink Friday 2*. The record debuted atop the Billboard charts and broke the record for female rappers with the most U.S. number-one albums, beating out one of Minaj's biggest inspirations, Foxy Brown. The album went on to continue breaking records, making Minaj the most successful female rapper in more than a decade.

The journey to greatness was not easy, but Minaj is a warrior. Celebrated and criticized for being bold and confident, Minaj takes life in stride. She infuses her songs with words of empowerment—words by which she lives every day, words that made the pink-loving little girl from Trinidad the undisputed queen of hip-hop.

Never Stop Learning

Throughout her career, Minaj has supported many charities and causes. One she is most known for is education. Minaj cherished her days at LaGuardia High School, and she's very vocal about the importance of education. Speaking to her fan base, proudly called "Barbz," in honor of Minaj's "Barbie" nickname, she once said, "You know what inspires me? Fearlessness, drive. Barbz, stay in school. Don't you ever be lazy; don't you ever complain about hard work."

Minaj puts her money where her mouth is, too. In 2017, she offered to pay college fees and student loans for her fans. She began with 30 lucky people, paying for

everything from school supplies to tuition, and promised to continue supporting her fans' education in the future.

Minaj also donates to a village in India. She's provided essential learning tools, such as a computer center and reading programs. In 2020, she returned to Trinidad to donate $25,000 to the St. Jude's Home for Girls. When she spoke to the students, she said, "I've experienced, you know, being at a very difficult crossroads in my life as a teenager. And sometimes as a teenager when things happen, you feel like there's no up from there." She shared words of encouragement and hope. "There [are] always better days ahead." Thanks to Minaj, many young girls at St. Jude's, as well as other institutions around the world, will continue to get the help they need when they stand at their own difficult crossroads.

First things first, all my girls, know your worth
Self-love is the greatest love on earth (yeah)
Cry your eyes out, get it out, it's the worst
But love don't hurt, no

—FROM "LOVE ME ENOUGH," FROM THE 2023 ALBUM *PINK FRIDAY 2*

SELECTED WORKS BY NICKI MINAJ

COLLABORATIONS

"Barbie World," 2023 (w/Aqua, Ice Spice)

"Say So," 2020 (w/Doja Cat)

"Rake It Up," 2017 (w/Yo Gotti)

"Side to Side," 2016 (w/Ariana Grande)

"Danny Glover," 2014 (w/Young Thug)

"Fly," 2011 (w/Rihanna)

"Make Me Proud," 2011 (w/Drake)

"Monster," 2011 (w/Kanye West, Jay-Z, Rick Ross, Bon Iver)

"Bottoms Up," 2010 (w/Trey Songz)

"Single Ladies Remix," 2008 (w/ Beyoncé)

COMPILATION ALBUMS

Queen Radio: Volume 1, 2022

MIXTAPES

Beam Me Up Scotty, 2009

Sucka Free, 2008

Playtime Is Over, 2007

STUDIO ALBUMS

Pink Friday 2, 2023

Queen, 2018

The Pinkprint, 2014

Pink Friday: Roman Reloaded, 2012

Pink Friday, 2010

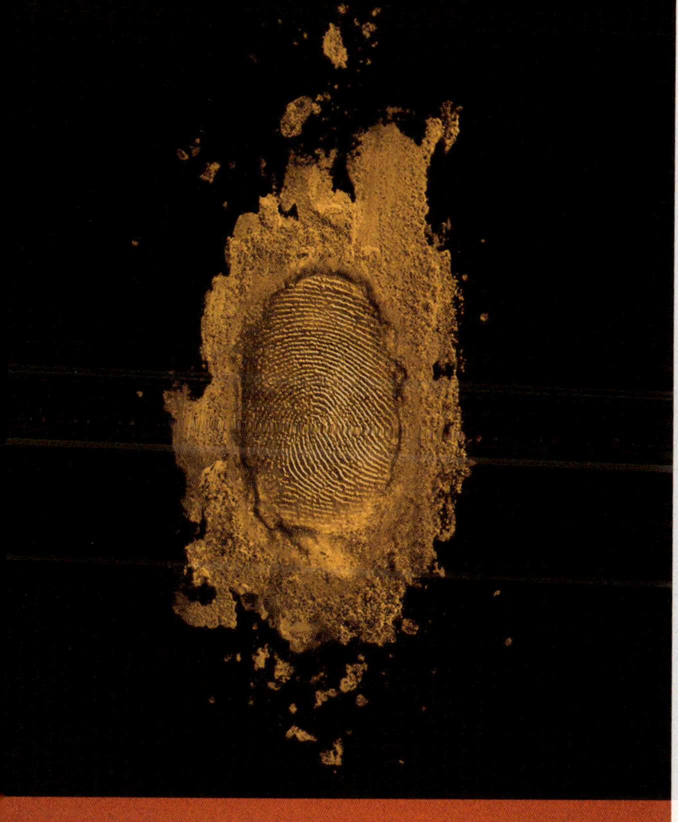

INDEX

albums

Pink Friday, 47

Pink Friday (Deluxe), 39

Pink Friday 2, 11, 43, 46, 47

Pink Friday: Roman Reloaded, 15, 17, 29, 41, 47

Queen, 34–35

The Pinkprint, 33, 34, 47

Barbz (fans), 44

Best Female Hip Hop Artist, 34

BET Hip Hop Awards, 11

Billboard 200, 29

Billboard Hot 100, 34

Dirty Money Entertainment, 24

documentaries

Nicki Minaj: My Time Now, 14

Fiorello H. LaGuardia High School of Music & Art and Performing Arts (LaGuardia), 18, 21, 30, 44

Grammy Awards (Grammys), 26, 29, 34

influences, 21

Lil Wayne, 23, 24, 25

Madonna, 26, 29

Maraj, Carol (mother), 12, 14, 17

Maraj, Onika Tanya (birth name), 12, 18, 29

Maraj, Robert (father), 12, 17

mixtapes

Beam Me Up Scotty, 24, 47

Playtime Is Over, 24, 47

Sucka Free, 24, 47

movies

Ice Age: Continental Drift, 30

The Other Woman, 30

Barbershop: The Next Cut, 30, 33

The Angry Birds Movie 2, 35

nicknames

Barbie, 11, 44

Cookie, 18

Papa Bear (son), 36

Petty, Kenneth (husband), 36, 37

shows

In Case You Forget, 21

Queen Radio, 34, 47

songs

"I Get Crazy," 24

"Love Me Enough," 46

"Moment 4 Life," 22, 25

"Roman Holiday," 17, 29

"Starships," 29, 41

"Super Bass," 39

"Super Freaky Girl," 43

"Win Again," 33

"Your Love," 25, 35

South Jamaica, Queens, 14, 36

Teen Choice Awards, 30

Trinidad, 11, 12, 13, 14, 26, 39, 43

Young Money Entertainment, 25